bodys

Kuhl House Poets
edited by Mark Levine and Emily Wilson

bodys

POEMS BY VANESSA ROVETO

UNIVERSITY OF IOWA PRESS, *Iowa City*

University of Iowa Press, Iowa City 52242
Copyright © 2016 by Vanessa Roveto
www.uiowapress.org
Printed in the United States of America

Design by Barbara Haines

The University of Iowa Press is a member of Green Press Initiative
and is committed to preserving natural resources.

Printed on acid-free paper

Library of Congress Cataloging-in-Publication Data

Names: Roveto, Vanessa, author.
Title: bodys / Vanessa Roveto.
Description: Iowa City : University of Iowa Press, 2016. | Series: Kuhl House poets
Identifiers: LCCN 2016007492 | ISBN 978-1-60938-455-5 (pbk) |
      ISBN 978-1-60938-456-2 (ebk)
Classification: LCC PS3618.O87253 A6 2016 | DDC 811/.6—dc23
LC record available at https://lccn.loc.gov/2016007492

For Diane and Joel

Acknowledgments

The following people have aided and abetted me in numerous ways. I would like to thank them.

Jason Livingston, Lesley Stern, Emily Wilson, Robyn Schiff, Donna Stonecipher, my workshop cohort, the staff at the Motley Cow, everyone at the University of Iowa Press, Molly Steiger, my siblings, Melissanthi Saliba, and most especially, Mark Levine.

bodys

These parts were written through patients against all hope for intimacy, the scream, a place, or love.

It was at the drinking fountain she met her. Between them, doughy tits extended over her stretched stomach. The husband and the friend poked while the camera held itself up to make an event. Reversing fortunes, the husband put a baggie on the baby's nose. Picture making in the time's frame, a genre of interruption. Someone knows something she didn't know about the inconvenience of other people. The sac sagged a close-up opportunity to prove itself. We were all avoiding the day her husband would be turning our videos deep into his secret. The two women smiled and smelled through the same socket. Melting, warm gusts over pores carving up sweat. The overhead lights picked up and left.

Why she laughed was because he was secretly thrilled. At the party, I had been mistaken for an object, a unit at which strong ends meet. Where does it sit, this jerkoffer that gets turned on while busting a broken ham underwater? The cold cuts tempted sweat, spilling over a mediocre facial. Every woman had become a community, communicable, a wounded sexual optimism. The soldier took no deli meat in the presence of such bald princesses, forgetting that gender war had been conflated with hairlessness. He had a most complicated vocabulary of feeling-your-feelings. That is why she laughed a second time, why I was without a multiplicity of choices. The forgotten boy spread his snout wide apart and buzzed.

She was entered. A mannered patient attitude working through hearse embraces, the shower eating her skin like a deadbeat. The woman-identified-woman refused to ingest her pills white, unblended. *For god's sake, pussy, when did you become conscious?* Her being awake modeled somebody else's pleasure and pinched hearts stopped in her spine. All of them playing the game, telling her the heads gave head, the blankets harbored the resentment of skinny sausage workers, of concentration clamps. The man wants the intern to know it's time to leave. Timing is appropriate in I'm Scared culture. Before the doctors, the brush had been a delicate pencil.

It was a show about a body. She obliged to provide a priest or a projection, admitting the pain of others was foreplay. Brain scans indicated the moral center and the disgust center overlap on the mind field. This woman, overconsuming, the bulimic stuck fingers down her throat. The eyes snacked easily, opening to the group's ball antics. There were clients that had chosen to be sterilized, practicing to love dispassion and the tension between unacknowledged cracks. I drove myself into a chewy embrace to hide the cold hearts that would later describe me. It was a bush with prescription and little remorse. After no contest, a canvas slices itself up, frays out.

It began as they moved into the ward, moved out of the would. He made a sound with her, balling up a cheese, putting their bodies into an incredible organization of one lump. They qualified at the end of a board game, cheering for bumps under her sweater. No skinless girl could corrupt their inadequacies, their patience cured and dried, savored by a pet ghost. Wrinkles backed by uncertainties named their mutual dislike for food systems they never understood. The mussels smiled while dying in butter. Their feed laid itself out while everyone's penises dipped into the pudding for proof. The ice cubes fetched a scenario as intimacy gave up on itself.

Cuddling parties, parts not getting inside. Her arms began to move away from her hands and made herself another drink. Lines of communication crossed a stroke. Lapping was a good sign here. As friends, lovers, as professional peers, we were challenged to find a balance. A woman in weakness reached for her bent body. She looked back at me and wagged barks. I lost track of my down-glance and forgot to separate bad beer from Not Even. Each abortion was a failed attempt to nourish our own and we acquired other means of taking care. There was a sweet brutality here in every nugget of oats, every utterance of animal.

She was very fond of them in the academy, in the asylum. She gulped as he reached on top of her and before she even knew it. I had nerve enough to stray, *This is the way I think sperm feels.* I found pill pushers provoking the anxious and yet they gratified with their presents of unzipped jeans. She needed a haircut, an algebra tutor. Desperately wanting to drop body fat, she forgot about touching herself because there was no use remembering to cry. For this was feudalism or something and there were no burritos. Hers was an initiative called Sentimental Value, featuring chew toys for excitable types. They were lions in love, all the women, a new bridal trend that made total sense. Larger than right.

Closing her eyes, accomplishments were divided by past aspirations and an index of unhappiness was acquired. Her good-enoughs were stacked up against a measurement of freshly cut pores. The result was a fraction of happiness attained by a standard of uncut skin. So many times I lost track of the long division, when she joined me in my stall to clarify the need for every human wanting to watch their meat. The time-sensitive woman moved without sentiment because after all a smile is nothing but a place that helicopters watch. The sweat locker was a meeting room, a tub. As they slithered into her, all their security numbers went cold.

All events were conjoined into each subsequent event, making room in the present. The gym is where the myth occurrences haunted one another. The diving board brooded loneliness like a dark bug archive, the bleachers thought about affairs of the heart, the soul, ice-cream licks. His sunscreen smell stuck on her head. Like a piece of mole on the ear that couldn't be tanned to make lamps smile. Time laps. Six and four years previous were indistinguishable from each other. Chronic chlorine killed vibes. My fingers swore cold, but warmed when greeted by interesting courses of seafood. It was not as if they would get impregnated, these men in towels. For the longest time, luck was not passed around at the tea party. No rabbits' feet, only the history of memory crystallized in a flipflop.

A girl slept in her bed. The father slept in her bed. Every household had its party members and no one could come unless they exploded the donkey pinata with a fork. Theory or not, this beast was a burden. I wanted to know where the closest dairy might be where I could suck and metastasize my ego. Being naked was only a myth, but not like all myths in that it was very real. Anxious, the doorknob was rubbing itself, opening its own keyhole, an aperture into the market. *Tell me if you like a fist full,* he slacked. The starched pillow, a kind of weirdo, begged only for recognition from a breathmint.

The question he asked was about feeling up several at once. He said it to draw something out of my age, just to see if I knew the difference between a bath and no shirt. Naked was a competition. Watching itself, her anxious pill had come to love its own bottle, producing a method. They didn't know how to adjust to the way she made space long but also long for. No matter where she went, the online thing scattered her opportunities to have fingers pointing to the place. This was the only option. He helped her holes and I helped her know how much. I liked a lot of people then, some in front of me, some that were offsite-specific to my appetite. My belly was like soft tissue that made napkins scared and stiffen. What was covering up his bad breath was this. Love was when the date ended.

She started writing this at 5 o'clock at night and it was still 5 o'clock at night. This first part of this was writing. The second part of this was rendering or remembering the same forms being made of many. She still makes this mistake, at least 5 seconds of extreme eye contact today. Downward, the shoes just wanted to know, *Why did your part freeze?* It got so stiff in this wet skin lacing up the mouth of my belly. Theories filling her up, there is no such thing as other people. Last night one of the girls asked about the relationship between a body and nobody. It was the beautiful question.

Her testimony went to the grocery store to buy tomatoes. She punched the fruit or the vegetable problem at its peak. She went to pay for the bikini and was charged for potatoes. Wanting desperate nourishment, she tolerated a something's off poker and was sure not to bother the surrounding others. Then she went home to cook the testicles and saw they were eggs. Watching, she realized she hadn't yet left the apartment, that her neighbors could be seen-heard saying that her wanting looked human. Later I thought I remembered that people have to undergo an internal change in order to be able to confront the existing social system. Luckily each member came with a silencer.

At the check-in line, there is one woman and there was another woman. They digested each other's desire in the money spending itself on sheets of hemp and heaps of shit. Their handbags stared, wetting themselves, the lipstick getting a sympathetic hard-on for the man watching their carrots peel away across the barcode. It was eyed by all the people in the store who had faces like too many bees. As the customers pricked fresh, the situation of whether or not they were hothouse twins or organic spirits was irrelevant because both women were the same persona. His favorite was mental disorders and tomboys.

An agitation of the felt heart caused a sound unworthy of pity. On boats, an order arose everywhere. The waves shook their sheath near our serious membranes and followed with a vacillation. The watching dolphin came closer and sniffed me, a fresh action on deck. No place was just one anymore. In the street, on the sore, in his hip. A woman who quilts penises and sells them was our hero. She stored a sliced-into tomato in his armpit that she couldn't finish. It was a woman who knows how to swim and eat with an undertaker's eye for caretaking.

One night he springs it on me and I remembered what it felt like to be slit and thrilled. An open crib into a spirit onesie. Across the room, he took eye-pleasure from the vagina, a kind of vacuum. Identification was hardly possible although the genitals were contextualized. He had finally met his match. *A limit is unmade when you clean up the periphery. A limit is remade when you make the bed,* admonished the one who spelled without remorse. My woman dreams skinned and I plucked his penis with my mouth so that all three of us could be better at meeting one another's eyes. Again and again we solved our problems with baby ash. *I have the weirdest boner right now* she spelled in time. After all was said and done, this yoga shelter was nothing but a showroom for the poses of headcases and dead people.

Opposite was a stranger with a familiar face. She knew my name and intimate details about the distance between my breasts, across the lengthening of my brain. The artist was a currency of plastic and platelets in pain. Panic took over my eyes and felt sticky in its dressing gown. I hadn't cunted so many short-shorts in one event. The medicine reaching its investment levels killed my person or persona. I wanted out of our bodies to just think about intimacy or something like sex. This thought consisted of a man traveling through her baby veins like a rude holdup captive in her woman.

They met at the restaurant over a shared loathing for what is happening or the weather. They were grateful for chances to stare, to say no to real estate. Times were dedicated to drinking wine, beers fearing her vaginal authority. The world they thought was safe was merely a surgical extraction. As easy as liberating ghosts from other ghosts, a multiplicity of haunted desires. No alternative still strangles the popular imagination and sometimes immobility gives way. *I can't talk but I love you*, she hackneyed. The salted almonds dilated trust, offering them a step-by-step guide to wooded kisses. The tablecloth forgot ultimatums, folded up the chairs and teeth, grinning down. Such generosity does not come around too often or what it means to leave someone in order to know someone.

They met in the library stacks. The combination of graduate student and prostitute could not be underestimated. Platonists stressed the incongruity between high and low. He smelled like burger and she like the pockets of sneaky hens. The book about a depressed pill dreamt of traveling the distance between used and anxious influence. Penile flatulence filled the silence. Against the wall against my back against playing with ideas Mom gave me before she got cozy with a small counterfeit face. It was the day my nose changed its shape, wanting to wear a conforming mask to sneak into openings. To do any genre.

Mom warmed, *Invest in everything together.* She couldn't retire until I reproduced her efforts. Every evening Brother visited in a family way. I was taught the value of commodity from this action. A gallery performance that considered many corpse painters at once. The traces of workers came after Brothering. She washed his underpants or how seams draw something out of another. That was not a sentence, but a text in a frame. One question they snacked was, *Could your body next time supply napkin and platelets?* It was a show-off process. The speed at which I ruined coherence increased because the investor met with the dollars of an other's patience. One example of being untitled is someone willing to tell you their object choice is about you playing yourself in relation to them as a face.

She told us she had a position. He disregarded key points of her and presented a similar one. His was a distorted version of her and could be established in several ways. He attacked her with a kitchen knife and concluded his position was the erect one. That sort of reasoning and attacking a version of a person failed to constitute an attack on the actual prostitution. It was a multiple choice answer to a whackjob. The scab masturbated her pain, turning to wood. In those days the blade slit the abuse left after each chopping cock.

His was a guess-what position to become more suggestive. Eagerly ordering the cocktail with growing anxiety, her mouth signs bearing its influence. He estimated she was a bit euphoric, this man poking for smashed bugs in the disarray. The coat walked her until she was ready to collapse. He arranged ritually, setting the curve of drool on the heel of the other. Her lips, this woman's nose perched on his forehead like a hangover. All I wanted was for us to smoke my lungs with air, give the class a reason to believe it could win the war. Mom was sitting in for both as he masturbated himself, threw the shower-cap at the window, unable to allow for dreaming. Together, my face swelling up like two girls, one cup, a robe spread so wide it drove itself to sleep.

She to him, *I'm pregnant. No, I'm pregnant,* he courted. The pauses birthed phlegm and ultimatums seized a silence. She and he and they were not in the same room when they sneaked in these sentences. The joining of the dialogue occurred later in my head, and in bedbugs eating it out. Crunching toes, I had a mutual dislike for people eating people. Optimism was a dirty thing for the shortest shorts. I adjusted my rage to the pleasures toward a hostility no one would fix or climb, harnessing fur kisses, filling up on girls. There was loss in this meal setup, this hard plate's hatred for a rimming. To be clear, I wasn't even her girlfriend but an accident running over a loose raccoon.

She argued on-set with a man wearing a red mustache. *This is an economic problem of sadism.* I put forward a hypothesis and he agreed to will this explanation into the image. I was no longer either this or Snapchat. No device could corrupt my inadequacies. At the end of the day the mirror neurons mimicked a horror movie spending time in a dungeon. Later bare, the disguise unmasked itself and the cumstain absorbed it onto a No Panty Zone. Who you are in relation to actors, what is the relationship to knowing what you know. The naked thing. The idea greater than the experience. Sending themselves to an end, neither cared for the wedges of cement, all shadowed. The knife held onto the effects of oxygen.

Our bonds equaled a negative sum, a solution. What was implied in every glass of wine was alcoholism. What was implied in every class of adultery was genitalia. A typical chain reaction exploding the drink from adult penises drinking all our liquid assets. I hedged my breasts, the notes unable to be changed in time to pack up and rest heads on, tails off. He compared the taste of sadist chips with children. Privates school meal, jerking off in pain the night Mom said she was drunkenly unscrewing his wife. Consciousness had become a plug trick.

Enjoy the kitchen floor for its sleek effect was an answer to the other's availability. First time the woman's boy, lapping at the daughter's trust. Second time feeling the quality of a downward look before a prettier child. There were enough clues in the story for us to reconstruct the dots. Education was an imprint. She generated, *Oh I know all about it.* We laughed because we were afraid to consider it for all its potential privilege. The girl's ass slumped and the hairs on the floor grew old. I couldn't stop eating pieces of pills in a dark voice that said I will never be a jazz singer, will dilute every stage with a pulse. The stupid things I said to her stayed there one hour more. Photo time, a time's frame, she wagered.

A text was sent to a mother with the words, *u were like a mother to me*. To be clear the woman was both and didn't have enough time to know. I knew we could count on unable men and that her meds ultrasounded a venereal ease. I couldn't remember the last time I imagined a woman who did this much speed or enlarged protrusions. My mother sitting on Facebook asking everyone who knew. Lump relations. Connection had grown into a dumb incest television.

Her girlfriend that night became the kind of barista who got stran-gled, the skirt hunting its own plaid. *Can we do some dirty thing before it's too late?* was tasked. It was too late. I was roped into an antagonistic pattern of thought and we didn't even know who we were talking. Foaming was no different than forming. The latte sweat blobs, its white coat shuddering as I was asked for a to-go mug to conceal the identities of paying with cash. He creamed to me, *Fuck this* or *Fuck, sis.* Later on, the sperm was taken out with the trash.

The bored jockstrap brought relief to those who exposed pink-tinged embarrassments to the all-male jerkoffs. On one level she was amazed he hadn't run off like a connoisseur who tested turds just to feel the humbleness breaking down into mush. Steam was not merely an attitude but an altitude. My legs resisting position while they were putting them in their place. The lockers had a gym-bag's desire for closure. The boy chewing the tiles searching for an edge to tips flush. The towel was put to rest. I didn't fit in much anywhere.

He couldn't get any peace because of pleasing. Helper, she was turning to sex to have an event. I asked to be taken to a rough place, going into stabs at the heart, drilling into the whole, a followup by a payer's due organs. She was unsure about this way, always in woman-loving-woman absorbent behavior. This is because bumped muffins last throughout eternity. Curtains were married before the toleration and the letters flowed from the yoke on her back. It was against her but is her because it just is. Wearing the costume of fresh culture to target us, this was his skin. When she opened oneself to danger. I knew that the tightest amount of dad in any given recipe was a has-been boner.

He suggested I inserted him so that in the future I might hit upon some truth. *There is no such thing as method,* she ran in a quick manner away. Anyway you can't hear your own screaming. Particularly when the voice inside digests its own reader, belching out of my self. Years later I accidentally put him in a porno and he discovered that he was a character I had shit in the mouth. Eating medication in a time machine, no personal history. She watched from her spot, her humanness a post or a posture. Everyone's voices like they came on bugs.

When we use the word *remember* we are always reminded of it. That conjuring of a memory and that member replicating itself. I said this to a woman I was trying to induce into my wave. The word *spermicide* was applied to the situation. Only the cause could fix the idea and I begged her sand to grind me while I was asleep. It was as simple as killing plants with a surfboard, but not easy. Her tits conked out from too many antidotes about strangling celibates.

She turned on my webcam. I studied her thrust menu closely to directly appeal to him. The pizza stick unwrapped itself with his hands. The mixture raised a serious implication and we sifted through emotions drawn from my experience to find those germane to the ingredients. A needing for bread, this Googled process of emotional understanding spent unstimulated. The collision of physical adventure and the adventure of ideas excited them doubly, costing once more. This had to be paid for. The forgotten ranch dressing, congealed and staring at me, a dried oregano's gift for deadly lingering. We agreed to be closer viewers of ourselves in translation.

The jeggings fucked her fiercely at the food court. The thighs firmed as the seams made their way into the build-your-own corpse salad, up the eyes of the security camera. *I wear my buckle to the side so that no one looks at my crotch,* she chained to me. I looked at her crotch. The mannequin sitting inside me set herself on fire and I watched it all happen from behind the cash register. She didn't want to think about his face, his beating bush, his boyfriend jeans or his kidney, the one and only one. Across the cry, a mall burrito unraveled itself, spilling the rice, the fake arm, the history of entering someone else's aesthetic project.

The dumper dove into heirloom pinto beans, giving meaning to forced entry or artisanal cancer. He couldn't figure out how to shape all the naked partyboys in trash-bags along the side orders of grease. Homeless bugs pandered for extra cheese, guac, the scent of strippers coated in salsa. Their pandering loss of control was rendered from the body's past, pondering the future tense of this state. The cook fucked the hostess with her pull quote and the enchilada came all by itself. It all took me back to that time I first loved woman sounding like man. Somewhere, chips fell out of an eyehole.

Slicking up the spandex, she hit me and I deserved it because I asked her to. The headband cried when it thought about cheating with a dream. He scissored the air and was munched out by a stereo with a voice whose victim was bugged. The process of us being fit was predicated on my experiences of watching an abused child or childhood. The story ended with a beating boxed up to look like the present tense. My best workout can eat anything, regardless of diet or dying. The gloves slipped into someone more comforting and sweat wept from upright palms. The floor was a therapist.

Wandering the beagle park, I told him it was a bad thing to want to assault a dog. A slutty insult. I wondered about these animals being cognitively entwined with us, forced to evolve alongside our leashes, our wrinkles and hanging tension built by unacknowledged patches of grass. It was a wonder we don't need speech. These were the puppies that looked like fried chicken. We agreed there was a shared kissy face between the wagging and a piece of ball. The collar's agent asked for its client to be harmed, charming capital. When we played out the rape fantasy, he asked that we be called *bitch*.

In it, she was drawn away from him, events putting them in the mouth. His father also gave him drink when he is 5 o'clock. The parents quarreled. At times excluded from the room because of his curiosity, he fantasied their mutual secret screaming. Her oral-anal fixations were responsible for the free towel's coitus rejection. They all wanted him to know he belonged in this place with no blinds, with no blind chambermaids. He was the steak hurt in the loneliness. Living people were informed organs, kissing into headless mannequins. *How worn did he look,* she outlouded.

Times were for medium blonde ashes. Her head was hijacked and it was terrorized using the standards of the type of girls who cut themselves to be young. An examination of the events leading up was being characterized as the groom fingerbanged the bloody one. There was an intimacy between them in sharing rituals of upsettingly fried locks, something appealing about a shelter filled with scalps and wigs. Afterward, she bought me a gift card for the future and I slid its purchase to change into something that vibrates on a button. Its charge was permission to leave my own body on the slab.

At 10 o'clock her heat put itself out while everyone else watched the girl qualify for a stroke. At 10 o'clock I took out the gun and killed him underwater. At 10 o'clock the grope mentality was reprimanded and time functioned like he loves it. A dissociation was formatted to make sure the victims unit focused on the plastic baggie, on all the other evidence of swimsuits taken beyond the edge. Their scrape kits collected pixels and I become an airborne gif. In both instances killing it was bad and also a present participle of the prime fist season.

The T-shirts power-walked their way through five trials, two missed periods, a slight depression on his crack. Growing like a forest's itch, hiking up was a vulnerable sport. She was sure that this city had cravings for the movement occupying itself in the sports bras of children who looked like girls. I stopped in the hallway path and smelled, *Democracy now*, an effort to spotlight my crotch with the armpits of politicians who snack it out. No journey was as winding as the infection making its way through the celebrant death canyon. My inner bump and cloth were in agreement. He said sorry in another demonstration.

The apartment victim quickly pushed the salmon away, just before using it to zip up his pants. That night and many after I was told my look of maturity was problematic. My mother made me peanut bumps, easing to me, *That's one lucky lady who won your heart.* No courting talk, real talk about souls for life is short and every moment is precious. Girls and girls in America go through a sad time together, dreaming about ponies who can't hear. In Escape culture we organize together. Dear men, she gave up. A below-job is relevant in that it occurred, if for no other reason. The woman who didn't love me sent me soft photos and I didn't sleep with him on my mind but her.

She said she's afraid men won't love her, what with her belly and no bellybutton after having the babies. *What is a belly without its bean?* All horror movies are about this thing, and about fisting fucking her, a second thing. The brother didn't feel bad about it, and the belt started therapy to loosen its desire to open a store selling veins. Waking up to men, things can be without their exits. She's hotter than she portrayed on TV, online and in electric chairs. There's something that can be said for faking her own death with his spunk. This made me laugh because it's so true.

You cannot teach a baby to commit suicide. He never really gets that far, I don't think. Community had become a *Look alive, every-body*. The thoughts shared in the active role of controlling the situation troubled the interaction. The therapist was confused with the Chair. Direct physical contact was downgraded, replaced with a counter. I was sitting on this person. *That's metaphor*, he spread. Or maybe, *That's what meds are for*. Rolecalling, the language started this whole awful thing.

Pole dancing was murky, made up of nonexistent referencing and rumors about gentleness. She spent some lady months as a universal student, using online systems to find the incredible history of stripping down to let us know how to live. A one-eyed witness asked when they entered the dance studio and could his circus gaze lead to gross contemplation. The ice cubes doted on a powerfully hairy ballerina. This bummed-out vagina, she looked like a giant cookie with two raisins. There was no reason to not live. The sensitive pole knew it was where function and dystopia set each other on fire. *You are a person,* he degenerated.

The school for art, brushing upon its rich history of auto-vaginal insertion. They applied to anyone by tonguing the architecture of the studious and drunkenly groping an engorged gallery. She mistook her action for that of the former artist, used the stroke as a dildo with two ends and none in site. Hand writing instruments altogether evacuated themselves from the curriculum only to be replaced by a preference for lens craft, for sentient cum. Only the ears of famous statues shunned class by not hearing the canned corpse screams. The canon's girlfriend crunched periods and read philosophy from coffin archives. The professor's hearse a ghost pollution.

The hostile windows opened on their own. The man who didn't love the girl sent hard photos and she performed without peace. The clean guests texted, dwarfing and harmonizing the will of the general. Their soft disks feared pussies in business attire and clam spit. Just being in the room, together we all played support and left it up to the judges to assess our stick in a bun. Nobody remembered the nooses of people and all the housewives, their testicles spent with missing. The bar stool questioned the dynamics shaping and moving the general historical condition. All weighted for the caress.

Disappointment filled her like a balloon bladder, spilling across the hopes she had malnourished during the long death drive. Something begins to look fishy, for there was something about this tall man disguising the beasts with his own ferocity. Early farming representing his state of surrender. The care of crops and stock, emerging markets live with bovine capital. The tablecloth folded up their uneaten weeds, condemning these dreaming in an endless state of tomorrow. Tinder had become tender, legal and lethal. The phone's indifference between reap and rape.

He started rebooting the relationship by munching the waitress, redistributing intimacies across a too-sick pea arrangement. The symbol of his dominance, the spork made a wry face at the sight of this stabbing into something more ethically ambiguous. The involuntary man's laughter was a show-off thing, an overstimulated replication of choosing her own adventure. She spent the 10 dollar gift card on a press release, a pressure that required no fitting, a real rupture-eraser. I took a deep breath and reminded myself that groin was necessary up here, that by only wishing I could feel her own breasts. His folly smelled like rum in a diaper.

Her velvety beetle buttons and a special something came into his nose. *It looks lovely on you*, she swarmed and ejaculated. Showing off, he was hiding like a bullet in cum, attacks on females and a young heavy dress on a wire hanging her. The borderline towel showed increased signs of homosexuality and the plastic horses aborted, all congregating in dense clusters of behavioral sinks. Human members lacking consensus because there was no agreement on what too many meant. This warming trend buoyed her up, threaded her away across the hallway right into an orderly, smashing her yams without marrying them. She forgot about the bruised insects and began having a wonderful time.

The man sent phonetic transmissions and did not meet her eyes. Wire sockets fearing the penile comic apparatus. Together we all played support and left it up to the other guests to stuff our baked bean holes. There was an inability to get lost and I thought this meant home. Watching someone, wanting someone so badly I believed in the truth-raising efforts of leg-spreads. Sadistic elements entered like a piece of fur inside the lip, smiling. The cleaning woman smelled, a genre of interruption. She made the consequences for being unnoticed known in the odd tasting water. No intercourse.

The man slipped secretly into the open door policy, restfully as all men overseeing an oral understanding. He needed three honey hams for each hand, plus fist for famine. Shitting herself, she slipped into his meal part like that time my mother's tail tipped her own stiffness, wagging into a girl's pup. *No one can count on weed,* she swarmed, thinking these people must belong to the runaround residence. The mug's emptiness conducive to concentration, the dessert questing for recognition from the tines of a fork. Her spine's scope for error so broad, its lack of maturity girl-spreading in the bikini's humidity. The selfie's acumen for childhood, I swam down so far he touched my own cosmic loneliness. Induced erections surfing on a wave washed over my sound castles.

She grabbed a towel and ran toward the field. Rerunning, all of them, the self. A threesome always half-sits, half-hangs. It is reported where anybody goes. I can't stop eating these ugly peanuts. The bases are suddenly aggressive, balls going farther than they ever thought possible. Her face was set, as if filled with enthusiasm for a therapeutic activity. His tie was an improvised device, a neck game. She imagined her bat stuffing him. She couldn't so she switched teams and imagined kissing the other woman's sound, the arm floating freely from her hands. He kissed his boner. She returned to a thought her mom barfed up, *How many ghosts can I see until I become the unnoticed goal?* Last night the woman asked what is the relationship between being tracked, the inability to get lost and making home. I feel her pain and it hurts me.

When she was going up she says it was like a front ear. The face-less tract home. Seeing, we both knew the body was a re-feeding situation, an oral aggression. We choked the texts to hear. *The thing never works*, she mowed. The thing is the only option out. We both knew when it is time to go back, when it was time to take pieces of means to measure our horny success. There were sad faces etched in this desk, erected to facilitate our yearning. She walked out onto the tension built by slippery fake grass, the plastic hair. This was a dream-home for weeds whacking her. Wearing a privilege mask to pray for openings. No hose could cement her when she left her chair. It was emptied, this creamed mirage. It was their second date for one to open her possibilities of being a woman in danger. The lawn hid its bees.

She sought for the fire exit, dependent upon her body's softhearted room for haunting. Life experiences not all about dimwits, control freaks, but feeding on babies that are not something to be bought. Nobody ever dies of overpopulation. An irreversible molecular attraction, caterpillar relations, a tentacular network embracing all the world and sucking greedily from thighs. An artistic perception, veins of input. She who tried to get the king's penis or bitch out a louder dynamism, this woman unknowing that gay media are not the best guarantee for originality or pregnancy. Here I was realizing I once saw my great aunt's lips, that they were blue and they were mine.

Both insane and an academic, her theory was an insertion practice. The parts had come to constitute the whole new life giving meaning. She interrupted to tell you about Napoleon. It was not about this member strangling the waitress, but about the present standing in for the make-your-own mannequin display. Forgetting was the fact the youngest girl sweats the man who wasn't alive or faking it. You remember her sign because you died, waved good-bye as she whispered a hello scare. Proving trauma was a revolution in the making, a thong-enabled woman resisted the prevailing values she does not cop-control. What had become clear was the construction of the past had become the past, and I was her own territory.